Four Sides of Feeling

Book of Plain Poems

Bobby J. Morris

In Awe

Softening Eyes   5
Clearing My Throat   6
Acquitted   7
Stepping Down   8
What's Not Here?   9
Clean Company   10
Flip It Inside-Out   11
Linked Arms   12
Love Pissed Off   13

As a Child

Justin's House   15
Akron, OH   16
Containment 17
Before Church   18
Like a Puppy   19
Can't Forget   20
Predicament   22
Relationships   23
Town on Mute   24
Afternoons   26

In Young Love

Stacked Checkers 28
Chin Up 29
Walking Around the Pond 30
Merry Go's 'Round 31
In the Fence 32
Good Luck 33
Our Faces Painted 34
Rebel 35
Sitting Together 36
All Mission 37
First Impressions 38
You Jousting 39
Crowned Civilian 40
Oh 41

With No Doubt

Hold 43
A Lecture 44
Country Club 45
Too Comfortable to See 46
Laying on the Couch 48
Antsy 49
Small Religion 50
Commute 52
No Thank You 53
Head Down 54

3

In Awe

Softening Eyes

Full of humanity
Can't get rid of it
Ask to be different
But always retreat

Tears tell me everything
Leave me in wonder
The fact I have this help
Makes path less scary

Tears tell me when I'm lost
Is a forgetting
Not proof that I am lost
As a creation.

Clearing My Throat

This dancing upon broken bricks
Either sin or of the saints
It brings me forward into you
Without changing up my past

I'll come to you with the color
That's tainted me with it's smell
I'll bring it like a tree it's leaves
All I thought I crucified

Will commit to my human
The human in each human
I'll come to you presidential
Together we'll make a stand

To drown in Jewelry made for me
Can't ask it to go away
What I've been keeping secret is
All the gold I have to say.

Acquitted

Every bubble I hid
And word I once swore
By sit on the tongue I hold
Out for you to see
The cracks no longer hidden.

How do I walk like this with
Smile? Drowning in
Criss-crossed torn apart core drunk
On limitations
I vomit everywhere yet
Remain holy in
Eyes of one who knows me best.

Stepping Down

Was above the typical
Tit-tat approach to problems
But didn't get anyone
To give up their arguments.
We drove home in the dark which
Follows loud events didn't
Need to mention the challenge
Affixed to human mission
Which simultaneously
Does not affect the untouched
Nature of failure and does
Not fail to make failure syn-
Onomous with the mission
Therefore worthwhile in that
There's nothing else to tend to —
When there's nothing else it makes
What's there pretty valuable
Even if it's what others
Want me to keep to myself.

At some point there's no point in
Being anything other
Than the set of limita-
Tions that define me.

What's Not Here?

I have nothing left
To be taken not
A smile I want.
Obliterated
In the face of my
Freedom
Asking my past if
He recognizes
Me.

My former glory
Is crying but my
Tears are flying out
Celebrating the
Waited for absence.

The sins you mention
Light they all contain
Join you in the truth?
Where are you going?
Face and hands we own:
Facts to rely on.

Our words are not lies
Breath not accident
We find ourselves in
The specifics of
Existence we will
Come to love the one
Clamoring inside.

Pull you from basket
Fall upon this beach
Ask to stay until
Your birthday party
Is over.

Clean Company

A thunder bolt
Charcoal so clean
Angelic source
Was placed inside
Limitations
To model them
To wear them in
In a way that
Doesn't ask them
To go away
Accepted boots
Lowly to not
Discriminate
Between any
Circumstantial
Evidence of
Our unquestion-
Able right not
To be questioned.

Flip It Inside-Out

You taught me the ballerina way, a buncha' sand in my fingers and a bit of hope, wondering whether our best attempts at living differently are just that - attempts - they don't get us out' the bucket in which the wealthy keep us as trinkets, "really good hearted people", to make their room feel dimensional — whether, at best, we become a wood book-end on their den's shelf.

We are another room. One which houses the wealthy's room, holds them like trinkets. You are the ballerina. They are not the crowd. You are the room. They are not your comfort. Do not pretend to be in their world. They are hardly in yours. Do not let them make you a trinket. Show them they are more than a trinket. Become our president.

Linked Arms

We can't get far from Earth
Sunshine we can't forget
It's in water and sin
And in the forgetting

I'll kiss you where it counts
The spot where your mind's fine
The only spot we need
But the spot sold the most

Don't buy gifts not made to
Prove to us we are free
Ask questions that bring the
Answers we're afraid of

Find all the proof you need
To choose no moment less
Than the one given us
In which we're all complete.

Love Pissed Off

The amount of strings I
Lay before you I wonder
If my help is needed
Birds 'ready know your name
People are used to you

Your kiss remains so close
To you, you don't give it to please
I asked you what you're wait-
Ing for and that's when you
Told me it's up to me –

"Love is given to the
One who is not asking
Why they should have it, if
You don't know how to give:
You're afraid to receive

The fact that you question
If there is enough in
It for me means you don't
Know the One who's giving:
I've never had to leave."

As a Child

Justin's House

Kix cereal spilled out
Justin played Nintendo calmly
I came in and out of focus
Unrecognized in the forest
Scared by the prominent TV
Waited for my sin to spill out.

His M & D smoking calmly
They came in and out of focus
Confident deer in the forest
Even got along with TV
Unafraid of their love spilled out
Didn't kick me out, calmly.

Akron, OH

Tony's birthday was a bust
No one showed, went boom
I collected the valuables
Didn't like Tony anyway
Bored me with his
Conservative approach
To childhood
I wanted truck and desert
Where there was none
Ohio could be romantic
The mayors, children
Who know what they're
Talking about.
Ran about with any friend
But Vince was the best
He too was dissatisfied.

Where did that revolution-
Ary of mine go?
When did I start fasting
And stop speaking —
Shutting up with an
Honesty that only comes
From belief one is not
Welcome?

Containment

Mama bought fantasy
Daddy bought depression
Passed on mutual reality.
Singular dreams
Covering treasure
In chests so
Personal and unique.
Embodiments too
Robust and foreign
To dip in and drink.

Before Church

No cushion in asking. Told to do away with requests. Tucked an artifact into the back right corner of my room. Wanted the dots in my body connected. Wanted order in contrast to disintegration by knife of anger no one could sheath, only wield against siblings less angry lest there be imbalance in whose body housed the brunt of my father's dissatisfaction.

He was in the back room laying in his own shadow as a more predictable alternative to the children waiting for an illustration on how to share the flowers wanting to come from beneath their skins to find the flowers of others. He let us become the dust in the corner he could keep his eyes on. Didn't want to lose a grip on the Ace of fatherhood, a delivery system of social immunity he could live on as he starved on belief he was the one human Earth could do without.

Like a Puppy

Left on the wood front porch to get
To know my limitations
To taste Eternal Torch so I
Could be an imitation

Invited me in when I had
Given up when more like them
Wanted me a less frequent pup
Wanted me one with stem

Ate food with my body small
Spoke with my lips and mouth small
Walked around with my steps small
Felt with my expression small

They were joke ready to bite
They were joy ready to hate
They were love setup to spite
A deadline without a date.

Can't Forget

Last time that I saw her she
Said "Stand on your tippy toes."
But she herself wasn't sure
About the path she had chose

Storm looking to be noticed
Traffic patterns meant nothing
Choreography practiced
Was Thanksgiving-Day stuffing

Had so much pain it smiled
Walked along in pain's mile
Pain rules after a while
It won't just sit in a pile

Lived and choked on its fire
Smoked and chanted its refrain
Sleep couldn't take the tired
Sleep can't cover up a stain

Spent waking days in its wake
Hearing the man's feeble cry
Much more than her kids at stake
Couldn't leave him if she tried

Liked it when he talked to her
She re-breathed his drunken breath
Her spirit once again stirred
Even if crazy if meth

Too long without memory
Chaos intrinsic to her
Without blood holding the past
Blood absolutely sure that

What she had seen was a sin
Her father's soul was not clean
In asking her to hold him
He'd took what she had as teen.

Predicament

Only one in my body.
A secret.
Was revolutionary.
Created tumult
In my parents' hibernation
Never underway
But always being disturbed.
My body
With chaotic effect
Standing
In exact position
It found itself.

Couldn't change the facts
Of my existence but knew
My absence had a better
Shot at keeping them
Asleep.

Relationships

No one said yes
To requests for them
Those who say yes,
The ones in the boat,
Have no boat
Don't care if you get
Their promise of the
Missing factor
For devotion exchanged
Only by those taught
They have no choice
But to beg.

Town on Mute

Limp in second grade
Sittin' empty spade
B ball hoop not made
In pieces it laid

I couldn't be found
Screamed but made no sound
Couldn't stop the round
To that yard was bound

Bell rang where to go
Day over who to show
Gas station low glow
My stone wouldn't throw

Somewhere else to be
He could hardly see
Me in his routine
Drunk on "to be free"

TV schematic
Day automatic
Set to no static
Town calm but manic

Cheat on Thanksgiving
Higher plane living
Seemed they were giving
Whole lot of sinning

Lined up with demand
Story 'bout this land
No blood of human
People who can't stand

America sick
No one healing quick
Need a magic trick
To loneliness lick

Maybe that's it must
In loneliness sit
Until no longer
A cause for blsht.

Afternoons

I wonder where your eyes go
The amount they're home is so small
I wonder if there's another Earth
I'm supposed to be on
If I'm the one
Separated from the Plane of Beauty
And that's why you can't see me
That's why you stare past me to a god
Who haunts your consciousness
Like a devil might
You drift past me as the parade
I an audience member
Not getting to grasp
What I need to know.

I'm still left questioning
If I have permission to
Be your son.

In Young Love

Stacked Checkers

Lightly slid from Heaven
Showed up no problem
I asked why you were sent
You kissed me and said

"Shut the fuck up"

Found my body in my
Body as I should
Where gods give me the right
To do what I think

The Ocean's cool with

Showed me to put my
Shoes on like this talk-
Ing from a place you found
That afternoon from
Which only you have rights

To bring the rain

Both at home putting us
In the equation
Meant to bring one and the
Other into the

Promised Land.

Chin Up

Why so embarrassed be-
Ing naked take
Off what you think is do-
Ing a favor

Who wants their holo-gram
Validated?
Want you in a state they
Cannot deny

A reference point to
Bounce back into
Their own unquestiona-
Ble lack of need.

Walking Around the Pond

Most beautiful woman I've met
Eyes only trained for you
They look elsewhere but see nothing
Come into focus for you

Don't know who made you with all this
Purity in your stem
I only lose this sight when drown-
Ing in my own waters

You are magnificently rep-
Resenting humans and
I too am wonderfully rep
Resenting the basics

If we can just land on the ground
Which proves to us we're here
I won't let your hand slip from mine
We'll document beauty.

Merry Go's 'Round

Baby keep prancing
Spring up into every
Place that is asking

Show ev ry moment
Which invites you in how
Wonder full it is

Baby you're the one
The all-one who is alone
And has all at once

We tried to be one
We were nearly one, almost
Were an al-so one

We are no longer
But let us sing of it in
Our dreams and thoughts of

One another.

In the Fence

I slept with you to see
Us overcome silence
The trucks barrel down but
You just walk right on through

Kisses make a dif rence
When not counting on a-
Nother when they mean no-
Thing then mean everything

Us, day before last
Laying on other lawns
Us together in bed
But both there all alone

Stuck in rooms we enclosed
Wearing clothes we hated
Demanding feelings we
Thought would make us not dip

Our kingdom must crumble
If new is to enter
If love not ricochets
Is what we're going for.

Good Luck

Don't mind if I
Never go home again
Got someone who
Is making my trees bloom

The one I know
She who sweeps to smile
Talks all things to
No one gardens to say

Land 'round you bru-
Tal you stand no clue flow-
Ers chant you though
You're what they have that's true

When you sleep go
Slow make branches reach down
Kiss which finds us
In dark's looked for in light

You can indeed
Smile, my baby
The army men
That were here have passed
And all that is
Between us is Time and
She gets to be
On our side.

Our Faces Painted

The braids in your hair Biblical
You don't know all the good in them
Doubt you are ever liable
Your duty is always freedom

You walk back on top your fam ly
Take cities you're in without care
You've already won handily
I say, take time to eat a pear

Night glory in cheeks surprise me
You sit at dinner table free
Ought to make plea to get a set
Up like yours in that Evergreen

Don't mind when you say you're tired
Or ask me if you have done wrong
I'll never set you on fire
The iron you wield is too strong

The land you've conquered is not small
The place you found from which to breathe
Is of quality saint would call
From up above not underneath

Your eyes do not spell out question
I run away from all that's good
I'm the clown 'forgot to mention
One in which your soul's understood.

Rebel

Baby doesn't know she's flyin'
How fast she's goin'
Speaks like queen of yesterday wants
'nother go around

Looks me in the eye sometimes in
Case I hadn't noticed
Whatever I feel is missing
I've forgot to look for

Makes music from pessimism
Sings it like a hymn
Knows more than any thinker of
What is life and death

She loves me around noon-time if
That's when her clock strikes
If that's when we are in rhythm
If our movements lock.

Sitting Together

Your face when you don't know
The soft joy running within it
Peaceful like gentle rain
It keeps the lonely garden lit

You lay your body down
Such that it brings the sky to you
Proof drama don't exist
Proof you already know the Truth

Your eyes move slightly down
As feeling is moving on up
Then they raise to meet mine
And that's when I know we're enough.

All Mission

She's a woman. She's a feat. A lasting mix of what can be dreamed.
Born pure of defilement, of anything that anyone would alter, a
woman of the clean air that births the myths we sing about and
keep going because of, who breathe the clean air back into our
choking lungs.

First Impressions

When we first met: you a drop
Of black satin cloth in my life
Opened me like gentle butcher
And pointed to us together

The plant you accidentally
Placed in my foundation forgot
Still sings of you who knows not of
The perfect notes which drop off you
Like sweat.

You Jousting

I kissed you not because
You didn't have knife
Kissed you because it would've
Been a sin not to

Angel in human form
Quarter in the tin
You we're an angel then
Since then more like king

All you do is make hints
Life unfolds simply
All takes place in a day
Miracles do that

You June Lus ana rain
You dust on wet dirt
Dance with me a broken
Others call that sin

Poets can't speak of you
They are all so small
Today and for how long
You smile at Truth.

Crowned Civilian

Who the hell are you babe?
You upon yourself
Who the hell thought of you?
Let you be yourself

Sweet afternoon pickin's
Flowers off your moves
Dust settling behind you
Like it wants to stare

Glory-Be Trinity
But I'd rather you
And the steps you take in-
To the Trinity

The path you
Kiss and choose
And breathe.

Oh

She pulled me in
As I resisted her
At the bottom
Of a storm finding us

She thought of me
As a perfect outlook
That answer hit
Me in the famil yar

There's no ledge I
Don't want to leave the wind
Hasn't landed
Me in what I'd call home

But saw you rest-
Ing where I ought to be
And wondered why
I live outside my door.

With No Doubt

Hold

We are made holy so we sing
Made big so we can spread the word
Not to die in our own arms or
To dance on down to some old haunt

If eyes are meant for lookin' out
If soul is meant for takin' in
Ought to stay in my bus and take
All the detours my road opens

Come down to where the basements plant
Where there's no goin' deeper down
Wait until Hallelujah calls
And says, "Bring the last hurrah."

Don't bother with who fall unto
The swords they manufacture
Dance 'round them back unto Glory
For who refuse to walk away.

A Lecture

Saw this human once
Talk to his own kind
From a pulpit
Gave them nothing
Of him
Gave them floods
Of things
He wanted to pass
By him
Looked at them...
They were the ones
To keep away
Sent floods of things
At them
At them
Saw him
Try to keep them
Away.

They had no choice
But to advance
They had no choice
But to advance
Flood behind them
Was too tangible
Was too dark
It had no space
It wasn't that
They wanted to
Advance upon him
He didn't have anything
They wanted
He didn't have anything
They wanted gone
He just was facing
The wrong way.

Country Club

Housing prices should drop in areas highly concentrated with men
and women who don't love each other but support each other's
dependency on familial and financial comforts: making good looking
kids, owning cars that don't get dirty, building homes big enough to
not feel small and getting jobs unavailable to the common human to
produce self-generating praise in lungs in case no tailored friend is
around who, because their life is relieving-ly familiar, can confirm a
lack of need to change. If the respect is siphoned out of activity that
makes it easy to avoid change we might solve the inequality
problem.

Too Comfortable to See

They wanna move to New Orleans
Wanna see about New Orleans
See if it will tickle them right
If it's the one to treat them right
Consider their plans, their plans
Drip morning coffee on their plans
Stay at home live inside their plans
To see if dreams won't alter plans

New Orleans is the perfect place
To live inside their dream –
"New Orleans is the place with no
Feelings, only dreams"
Will go and get what they need and
Not notice anything
Will go and breathe its air and not
Have to leave anything

Will go and get what they want then
Return to comfort zone
Will extract nicely with a smile
A mine-as-you-please zone
Will go back home with only a
Slight sense of disturbance
Wondering if in the people's eyes
There had been disturbance

If they'd just dipped their toe in a
Pond who feels everything
A soul so great so ancient if
They had missed everything
If they'd just masturbated in
The home of a Teacher
If they'd just missed the chance to stop
Looking for a Teacher

Now back sitting in their home of
Thin supportive comments
A world made of who have privilege
To live on such comments
Nothing's actually needed
Only considered cute
World where the best things get is cute
World of cuteness lots of
Cuteness no connection to sin
Can't touch the floor beneath their dreams
Where others feel their sin.

Laying on the Couch

You're involved because you want more. If not injected with America's needle you wouldn't give a damn about dramatics. You're in its bed screaming for a never ending flow of topics to drown in lest you are alone with the self you have stuffed in the top cabinet, the planet you ignore, as you claim responsibilityless-ness, as you claim the problem is in the news.

Antsy

Went to bed last night
Thinking of the times
You told me I'd be
Plenty if I drank
The pales of water.
They were all empty.
Of the times you told
Me to believe when
You did not believe,
Demanding belief
As love condition.

I fell, fell to
A point above you.
You settled into
Hardening belief
In not admitting
We were crushed shapes and
In this denial
Try and steal the crown.

Do not be so strong
There is someone be-
Neath your feet strong so
Give it your whole weight
The Planet is big and
No one is *really*
Depending on you.

Why not join the fish-
Es in not doing
Anything you do
Not know how to do?

Small Religion

We keep god silent
We defend his cave
And say,
"No one's allowed in."
We refuse entrance
Into the land of Jehovah
Lest we be
Outside-the-gates
We refuse entrance
To the land of Jehovah
So we're closer
To the gates
Than the others.
If we defend the gates
We will have
Beach front access to it
If we can't go in
To Jehovah's land
It's as good as it gets —
Be the champions
Of his land
Of his kingdom
Of its gates
Be the champion
Of god's kingdom
Refuse entrance
To its gates
Defend the gates
Isolate god
Protect god
As if God were
Some fed up
Slightly guilt-ridden
But comfortable god
The god of Netflix

The god of taking showers
In his hotel room
The god of clean satin sheets
Clean-satin-sheets god

God, why do you care so much about the sheets?
God, why do you ask us to protect You?

This can't be so.
We take it upon ourselves
To defend god
To turn our backs
As if to take god
Under our wing
We turn our backs
And claim to be servants
To be followers
With backs turned
Speaking for god
Keeping god away
From God's people
We hide god
We claim god's
Inaccessibility
God's specialness
We claim god.

God. God. God. God.
Claim us!

Commute

A polished pair of pants
Is as good as it gets
In a good job.

Good jobs are the worst
They make what's good
Not matter and thus
We do not devote ourselves
To good things which
Because they are good
Only open up to
Those who's attention
Is not going anywhere.

Devotion's gone
Devotion's overrated
In good job psyche:
"Devotion is an
Unnecessary inconvenience
Why devote yourself
To The Loves of this life
When you have a good job
And polished pair of pants?"

No Thank You

Was good at being one of you
But was lifted by my collar
Away, let out on parole
Pulled back to corner of the ring
Where the doctoring happens
Where I know after out-of-breath
Rounds I've no association
With what you call our family.

What you're calling our family
Is a conference of abuse
Needing a life long pilgrimage
Of healing to come back to the
Vineyards of calm going on all
Along.

At that point let us talk about
Making a family when it's
Not excuse to tell each other
There is not a point in changing.
Until then, please stop texting.

Head Down

These days meant to not discover
To make it through without seeing
To stay within the shroud of lie
Lest Truth bring us back into Its
Fold lest we disappear into
The Love from whence we have escaped:
An isolated fetus
Swimming outside of its maker.

These days meant for that: running
For claiming an independence
In jail so drenched in dependence
A heart beat lived without even
Questioning the surrender lodged
Into our daily rhythm to
A life lived without surrender.

Bobby J. Morris

Studied at Franciscan University in Steubenville, Ohio; worked at BlackRock, a financial services company in New York City – co-founded BlackRock's team for Impact Investing. Hosts the YouTube channel, "Good Tiger Melody", and as "rJm3" wrote and produced the album, "Four Sides of Feeling". Video and audio work available at www.PoEngineer.com. Instagram: @bobbyj.morris

Gratitude

Thank you to each of you who have been around me and supporting as I've stumbled in the direction of writing - Joe C., Jack Epler, Ben Sahl, David Brunetti, Charlie Smith, Todd Stevenot, Barbarba Bash, Stanford Brent, Lyle Ashton Harris, Kris Gerig, Jeff Rodman, Tim Lee, Scott Trulin, Vegan Aharonian, Carl Eifler, Fr. Tim Danaher, Lucas Kovacevich, my sister Annie, all of my Shambhala loves and friends from Pasadena and New Hampshire Ave.

And thank you to all the places-as-hosts - New Orleans and Arabi, Lousiana, Artscape Gibraltar Point, (Kai and Ryn) Casa Werma and Patzcauro, Los Angeles, 1046 and Vermont Square Library.

Thank you to Janet Levin for being my first reader. And especially, thank you, Ed Taylor, for your kind and clarifying feedback while I tried to edit.

For
Sophia Bruno – thank you for your love and unforgettable take on things.

Printed in Great Britain
by Amazon